Original title:
Scars and Smiles

Copyright © 2024 Swan Charm
All rights reserved.

Author: Liina Liblikas
ISBN HARDBACK: 978-9916-89-895-6
ISBN PAPERBACK: 978-9916-89-896-3
ISBN EBOOK: 978-9916-89-897-0

Grace Amidst the Broken

In shadows deep, where hope has fled,
A gentle light, where tears are shed.
With every crack, a chance to mend,
Grace flows through hearts, our hands extend.

Though weary souls in darkness weep,
A whisper stirs, a promise deep.
In every fall, a rise we find,
The strength of love, forever kind.

Ascending from the Abyss

In depths so dark, a call resounds,
From silent voids, where yet hope bounds.
With faith as wings, we rise anew,
From pain to light, a journey true.

The heav'nly path, though steep and long,
Guides weary hearts, where we belong.
Each step we take leads us above,
To realms of peace, to endless love.

Echoes of Suffering and Laughter

In trials faced, our spirits blend,
With laughter born, where sorrows end.
In every heart, life's song resounds,
A melody of joy that surrounds.

Amidst the storm, we find our grace,
In joyous tears, we seek His face.
With every smile, and every sigh,
In harmony, our souls shall fly.

Divine Imprints on the Soul

In silence deep, His whispers flow,
Through every breath, His presence grow.
The marks of love, etched on our hearts,
In each glance shared, creation starts.

A tapestry of grace unfolds,
In every thread, a story holds.
Through trials faced and battles won,
Divine imprints shine like the sun.

Verses of Light in Gloom

In shadows deep, Your grace shines bright,
A guiding flame through darkest night.
With every tear that stains the ground,
Your loving hand brings hope around.

The whispering winds carry Your peace,
In silence, doubts and fears shall cease.
Each step we take, You light the way,
Transforming dusk to break of day.

Amidst despair, Your love does bloom,
A garden bright in direst gloom.
From shattered hearts, You weave anew,
A tapestry of love so true.

In every soul, the light abides,
Through trials, faith our joy provides.
With open arms, You welcome all,
To rise with You, we hear the call.

A Symphony of Healing

In brokenness, Your music flows,
A melody that gently grows.
With every note, our spirits rise,
In harmony beneath the skies.

The rhythm of Your tender grace,
Restores the weary, finds a place.
Each heartbeat sings, a soft refrain,
In sorrow's wake, You ease our pain.

Through trials vast, Your light does weave,
A symphony of hope, believe!
With faith as strings, and love the tune,
Together we shall dance by noon.

Beneath the stars, we join our hands,
In sacred unity, love stands.
As heart to heart, our voices blend,
A testament that will not end.

Cherished Echoes of the Past

In memory's hold, we find our peace,
The echoes of love shall never cease.
From whispered prayers that floated high,
We gather strength as days go by.

Your presence lingers in every heart,
In sacred moments, never apart.
Through trials faced, and joys unveiled,
Your guiding light has never failed.

The stories told by fireside glow,
Of wisdom shared, in every flow.
A tapestry of days gone by,
Each thread a gift, a sweet reply.

In laughter shared, and tears once shed,
We honor those who brightly led.
With open hands, we seek to learn,
From cherished echoes, love shall burn.

Dawning Over Shadows

As dawn breaks forth with colors bright,
The night's embrace gives way to light.
Your grace, like sunbeams, warms the cold,
In every heart, Your love unfolds.

The shadows flee at morning's call,
With every step, we rise, we crawl.
Your promises, like flowers bloom,
In gardens rich where hope finds room.

With gentle hands, You mold our fate,
Transforming loss to something great.
Through every trial, we've learned to stand,
In unity, we join Your band.

As morning stirs and fears depart,
Your light illuminates the heart.
In faith we trust, our spirits soar,
With every dawn, we'll seek You more.

Lanterns from the Shadows

In the night where fears reside,
Faithful hearts search for light.
Lanterns flicker, shadows glide,
Hope ignites amidst the fright.

Every tear a prayer's embrace,
Guiding souls through darkened paths.
With each step, we find our grace,
Brightening the aftermath.

Wisdom whispers in their glow,
Carving purpose from despair.
In unity, our spirits grow,
Lanterns cast a loving care.

Together we brave the storm,
With courage born from love's fire.
In the dawn, our spirits warm,
We rise, as hearts conspire.

Faithfulness Amidst the Fray

When trials surge and voices clash,
In the chaos, we hold fast.
Faithfulness is not a rash,
But a beacon meant to last.

Every doubt a silent plea,
Strength is found in unity.
Amidst the fray, we will see,
A tapestry of harmony.

The footprints of our past reside,
Encouraging our hearts to trust.
With every heartache, we abide,
Bound in love, we shall adjust.

Trusting in the hand divine,
Guiding us through every storm.
In our hearts, a sacred sign,
Faithfulness will keep us warm.

Spirit Wounded, Love Renewed

In the depths where shadows creep,
Wounded spirits seek to mend.
With every tear, a promise deep,
Love's embrace begins to blend.

From the ashes, hope will rise,
Hearts entwined, they bear the weight.
Through the pain, we learn the wise,
In love's arms, we cultivate.

Forgiveness blooms amidst the hurt,
Tenderness breaks through the night.
Where once there was the bitter dirt,
Love renews with gentle light.

Together, we weave our tales,
In the heart of every storm.
With each shared breath, love prevails,
As spirit finds its way back home.

The Veil of Trials

Behind the veil, a lesson hides,
Each trial shapes our fragile hearts.
In the silence, hope abides,
Healing starts where faith departs.

Through the struggles, we unite,
Hands entwined, we lift our gaze.
In darkness, we find the light,
Igniting love in endless ways.

Every struggle, a sacred thread,
Weaving strength from pain and strife.
In our hearts a spirit fed,
Emerging with a brand new life.

Together we shall face each test,
Filling voids with grace and cheer.
With faith as armor, we feel blessed,
Through the veil, we journey near.

Light Emerging from Darkness

In shadows deep, a whisper calls,
The dawn breaks soft, as nightfall falls.
A single spark ignites the way,
To guide our hearts, to greet the day.

From silent depths, we seek the light,
A promise born in endless night.
With every step, our spirits rise,
To pierce the veil, to touch the skies.

In trials faced, we find our truth,
In faith restored, we find our youth.
So lift your gaze, embrace the flame,
For love and hope shall never wane.

Through darkest paths, we walk anew,
With grace bestowed, our vision true.
Embracing light, we lose the chain,
And find our peace, through joy and pain.

The Resurrection of the Soul

The tomb is bare, the stone rolled wide,
In silence reigns, the life inside.
A breath returns where death had claimed,
Awakening hearts, now unashamed.

With outstretched arms, we seek to fly,
To heaven's gate, beyond the sky.
For every sorrow lays the ground,
For joy reborn, in love profound.

From ashes vast, the spirit soars,
New life ignites, forevermore.
In darkness met, the light we hold,
With courage bright, our stories told.

A victory won, our faith the key,
To open doors, to set us free.
With hope renewed, we rise within,
To dance in grace, where life begins.

Chronicles of Courage

In battles fought, with hearts so brave,
We stand as one, our lives to save.
With every scar, a story known,
Of faith unyielded, love has grown.

Through raging storms, we hold our ground,
In whispered prayers, our strength is found.
The echoes call, through ancient times,
In unity, our spirit climbs.

With every fall, we rise again,
In trials faced, we find our gain.
The path is steep, yet we press on,
For in our hearts, the dawn is drawn.

With courage fierce, we break the chain,
In every heart, a spark remains.
Together strong, we face the fight,
With love as shield, we claim the light.

The Pilgrimage of the Heart

A journey starts, with steps of grace,
Each mile we walk, our fears embrace.
In seeking truth, our spirits gleam,
Through valleys low, to mount the dream.

With every turn, a lesson learned,
In silent prayer, our souls discerned.
The road may twist, the path may stray,
Yet love's soft hand will light the way.

In gatherings shared, we find our kin,
A tapestry of heart within.
With open arms, we share the load,
For every heart, a sacred code.

So onward still, our voices merge,
In harmony, let spirits surge.
In faith we walk, through joy and tears,
The pilgrimage unfolds through years.

The Sacred Dance of Wounds

In shadows deep where sorrows lay,
The heart does pulse, a rhythm sway.
Each wound a step in sacred grace,
In pain, we find our sacred space.

With every scar a story told,
A dance of light where spirits bold.
In unity of broken dreams,
We rise, we fall, in holy themes.

The tender touch of love so pure,
In wounds, a bond we must endure.
Together we weave through the night,
In sacred dance, we seek the light.

From ashes born, our spirits sing,
In every wound, the hope we bring.
Through trials faced and battles won,
The sacred dance has just begun.

So let us twirl in joy and pain,
With every tear, we break the chain.
In love's embrace, forever blessed,
In sacred dance, our souls find rest.

Threads of Forgiveness

In the loom of life we weave,
Threads of grace we must believe.
Forgiveness shines in darkest night,
A tapestry of purest light.

Each thread a prayer, a whispered vow,
To mend the heart, to heal the now.
In tender whispers, love resounds,
Through every wound, a grace abounds.

We gather strength from storms we've faced,
In every tear, our fears erased.
The fabric strong, though frayed it seems,
In every stitch, we share our dreams.

With every heart that we embrace,
We find the light, we find the place.
The threads of love, the threads of peace,
In forgiveness, our strife will cease.

So let us weave with gentle hands,
A world united, where love stands.
In harmony, our spirits blend,
With threads of grace, we shall transcend.

Offering Joy from the Abyss

In darkest depths where shadows creep,
A flicker of light, a promise deep.
From caverns cold, we rise anew,
In joy we find the strength to pursue.

The abyss whispers in tones profound,
Yet hope awakens with each sound.
With open hearts, we greet the dawn,
In every trial, new life is drawn.

The burdens borne, we lay them down,
In joy's embrace, we find our crown.
The struggles shape the soul so bright,
From depths unseen, we chase the light.

With every laugh that fills the air,
We rise above what once was despair.
In gratitude we lift our song,
From the abyss, our spirits strong.

So let us dance on highest hills,
With joy that bursts, our spirit fills.
From every sorrow, joy we reap,
In offering love, our souls shall leap.

With Every Tear, a Revelation

In silent moments, tears do fall,
Each drop a truth we hear the call.
Within the ache, a lesson clear,
With every tear, a revelation near.

The heart laid bare, the spirit bared,
In depths of sorrow, love declared.
Embrace the pain, the joy it brings,
In every tear, the wisdom sings.

From grief, a garden starts to bloom,
Each tear a seed, dispelling gloom.
In cycles of loss, we find our way,
With every tear, a brand new day.

So let us honor what we feel,
In vulnerability, we heal.
With every tear that falls with grace,
A revelation, a sacred space.

Together we traverse the night,
In every tear, we seek the light.
With open hearts, we dare to see,
The beauty in our fragility.

The Soul's Testament

In shadows deep, my spirit sings,
A quest for truth, the heart it brings.
Through trials faced, I stand so tall,
With faith as guide, I answer the call.

Upon the path where mercy flows,
The light of grace forever glows.
In whispered prayers, my burdens lift,
Eternal love, the greatest gift.

In silence, hear the soulful cries,
Transcending pain, the spirit flies.
Each tear, a pearl, a lesson found,
In unity, our souls are bound.

In every heartbeat, sacred trust,
Through darkened days, we rise, we must.
With open arms, we receive the flame,
In hope we dwell, in love proclaim.

Thus, my testament, a story shared,
In every struggle, love has dared.
Together we walk, the journey true,
In heart and soul, I find the new.

Mosaic of Blessings

In tender moments, blessings bloom,
Like stars above, dispelling gloom.
With gratitude, our spirits soar,
In every breath, we seek and explore.

Each heart a piece, in colors bright,
Together forming the sacred light.
In every smile, a story's told,
In unity, our lives unfold.

Through trials faced, we rise anew,
With hands entwined, we push on through.
In laughter shared, a joy divine,
In every moment, grace we find.

The ebb and flow, the dance of fate,
With every heartbeat, love won't wait.
In silence found, we hear the song,
In every soul, we all belong.

Thus woven threads of faith and cheer,
Together bright, we conquer fear.
In every heart, a radiant space,
In life's mosaic, we find grace.

Embraces of Hope

In twilight hours, hope takes flight,
A tender embrace, the darkest night.
In every sigh, a whisper near,
In faith, we stand, with hearts sincere.

When shadows loom, and doubts arise,
In prayerful hearts, we reach the skies.
Together strong, we face the storm,
In love's embrace, we find our warm.

Through valleys low, and mountains high,
With every step, we dare to try.
In hands united, we journey forth,
In shared resolve, we bring the worth.

Each story written in sacred ink,
With every tear, we learn to think.
In trials faced, our spirits rise,
The light of hope, our faithful prize.

Thus, in each moment, we hold dear,
A beacon bright, to guide us near.
In life's embrace, we find our way,
In hope's sweet arms, we choose to stay.

The Gift of Endurance

In weary nights, the spirit shines,
With every burden, love entwines.
Through trials faced, we rise from deep,
In whispered prayers, our dreams we keep.

With open hearts, we greet the dawn,
In every struggle, we are drawn.
Through tempests fierce, our will stands strong,
In every test, we find our song.

In moments fleeting, time reveals,
The courage found in faithful seals.
In every fall, we learn to rise,
Endurance grows in humble ties.

With every challenge, lessons flow,
In paths unknown, in faith we grow.
Through gentle hands, we lift each other,
In every struggle, we find a brother.

Thus, let us rise, with spirits bold,
In every story, love's truth unfolds.
In endurance, we breathe anew,
The gift of life, forever true.

Heaven's Wounds and Glorious Grins

In the quiet whispers of the night,
Love pours forth, a gentle light.
Heaven's wounds, they breathe and sigh,
Glorious grins in the softest sky.

Through trials borne, the soul is dressed,
In garments stitched by faith's own quest.
Each tear, a gem of grace bestowed,
In the heart, a radiant road.

From shadowed valleys, hope ascends,
Eternal truths where sorrow bends.
Amidst the ache, our spirits rise,
To touch the beauty in the skies.

The broken roads we walk each day,
Lead us gently to a brighter way.
With every scar, a story shown,
In love we find we're not alone.

So lift your eyes and seek the morn,
From wounds of heaven, joy is born.
With glorious grins, we face the day,
In faith and love, we find our way.

The Alchemy of Pain and Joy

In the forge where trials blaze,
We discover love's sweet ways.
Pain and joy, a dance so pure,
Through the fire, our hearts endure.

Like gold refined in flames of fate,
Every moment teaches great.
From bitter roots, sweet fruits will grow,
In the silence, love's light will show.

With every tear, a lesson learned,
Through the struggle, the spirit yearned.
In the darkness, hope will bloom,
Where sorrows turn to joy's perfume.

Embrace the shadows, welcome light,
In the sorrow, find your flight.
The alchemy of soul and dust,
Turns the frail to bright, we trust.

So sing of pain and joy combined,
In every moment, grace aligned.
Transform our trials, share the song,
In love's embrace, we all belong.

Celestial Marks of Faith

In the morning light that breaks,
A canvas painted with our stakes.
Celestial marks upon the soul,
Remind us of our greater goal.

With every heartbeat, faith does swell,
In shadows cast, we cannot dwell.
The stars above, they guide the way,
Through darkest nights to brightest day.

In whispered prayers, our hopes ignite,
Through trials faced, we seek the light.
Each scar a testament, so clear,
To love's embrace, we draw so near.

With every breath, our spirits rise,
To meet the grace that never dies.
Celestial marks, so profound,
In every heart, His love is found.

So let us walk with faith as guide,
With open hearts and arms spread wide.
In unity, we share the call,
To love each other, one and all.

Light Emerging from Darkness

In the depths where shadows lie,
A flicker sparks, a fervent sigh.
Light emerging from the dark,
In every soul, a sacred spark.

When trials weave their heavy chain,
Resilience shines through all the pain.
From ashes rise, a phoenix true,
In lost moments, we find what's new.

As dawn breaks clear, the night must wane,
In every loss, there's much to gain.
Hope's soft whisper fills the air,
A promise made — we're not in despair.

The rhythm of the heart beats on,
In every struggle, love's not gone.
Light emerging, unfurls the grace,
That fills the void, our hearts embrace.

So walk with courage, face the strife,
For every ending births new life.
In darkness deep, let joy reside,
With light emerging as our guide.

The Serpent and the Dove

In shadows deep, the serpent hisses,
With whispers of doubt in the dark's abyss.
Yet, purest doves in radiant flight,
Bring forth the dawn and dispel the night.

In trials faced, we seek the light,
The dove ascends, soaring in height.
With gentle grace, the truth is shown,
While serpents slither, seeds are sown.

With every fall, a rise is near,
In every whisper, a voice so clear.
Through faith, we find our golden path,
Turning our hearts from wrath to wrath.

The serpent coils, but love prevails,
In the heart of dusk, hope never fails.
For every wound, there comes a balm,
In heaven's arms, we find our calm.

So trust the journey, let not fear bind,
For in the struggle, the soul we find.
Emerging stronger from trials we face,
The serpent is quelled, the dove's embrace.

In the Garden of Redemption

In tranquil fields where lilies bloom,
Past shadows cast, dispelling gloom.
A gentle breeze, a whispered prayer,
In the garden, love lingers there.

With every seed, a promise sown,
In grace, our deepest wounds are grown.
Through tear-stained soil, new life shall rise,
In the garden, the heart complies.

Amidst the thorns, the rose blooms bright,
A testament of hope and light.
With hands in earth, we toil and strive,
In unity, our spirits thrive.

The harvest waits, with joy we glean,
In every shadow, His hand is seen.
For from the ashes, beauty springs,
In the garden, salvation sings.

Let those who wander find their way,
In love's embrace, we choose to stay.
For in redemption, we are made whole,
In the garden, we find our soul.

Joyful Tribulations

In trials faced, a song we raise,
Through darkest nights, we seek the praise.
For every storm, a lesson learned,
In joyful hearts, the fire burned.

In suffering, a strength unfolds,
A story written, hope retold.
Through pain and strife, we find our song,
In every battle, we grow strong.

The path may twist, the road may bend,
Yet, love remains, forever our friend.
With joy we journey, hand in hand,
In tribulations, together we stand.

The dawn will break, the sun will shine,
In every heart, His love divine.
For in the pain, we find the grace,
In joyful moments, we seek His face.

So let the trials come and go,
For in our hearts, His love shall flow.
In joyous laughter, through tears combined,
In joyful tribulations, peace we find.

From Ruins to Revelations

In shattered dreams, the heart does weep,
From crumbled hopes, the soul takes leap.
Yet in the rubble, light breaks through,
From ruins found, new life anew.

In ashes stirred, the Spirit breathes,
In brokenness, a heart believes.
With every heartbreak, strength we gain,
From ruins rise, through joy and pain.

The stones once cast, now pave the way,
To revelations bright as day.
For in the depth of our despair,
We find the grace that lingers there.

The past may haunt, yet hope transcends,
With every step, our journey mends.
From ruins built, a vision clear,
In faith, we stride, casting out fear.

So let us rise, like phoenix from ash,
With every moment, let's make it last.
In revelations, His love's embrace,
From ruins to grace, we find our place.

Paradigms of Aspiration

In silence, dawn awakens hope,
Each dream a step toward the light.
With faith as our guiding rope,
We rise, the dark fades from sight.

Hearts lifted high, spirits whole,
Every challenge a chance to grow.
Beneath the weight, we find our soul,
Through trials, the seeds of love sow.

With every breath, we seek His face,
In humility, we find our song.
For in the struggle, there is grace,
A journey where we all belong.

Together, we'll build a bridge,
Connecting earth to the divine.
With every word, we honor a pledge,
In unity, our spirits intertwine.

Let light pour forth from every heart,
A symphony of voices clear.
In this, we each play our part,
Collective hope, with none in fear.

Hope's Fingerprints

In shadows dark, a whisper gleams,
Hope's gentle touch on weary night.
Through cracks of doubt, the sunlight beams,
A promise born from inner light.

Each step we take, a new refrain,
The pulse of faith in every stride.
In joy and sorrow, love will reign,
With hope, we turn the tide.

The world may judge, but we shall rise,
With scars that tell a story true.
In every tear, a glimpse of skies,
Reminding us of what we knew.

Together, we will journey far,
With hearts ablaze, we'll share the way.
Each act of kindness is a star,
A beacon bright that will not sway.

In hands outstretched, a prayer of praise,
For all the paths we've walked before.
With every dawn, the spirit stays,
Hope's fingerprints empower us more.

Celestial Rainbows over Tempestuous Seas

In stormy depths, a light appears,
A rainbow graced by heaven's hand.
Through trials fierce, dispelling fears,
Guided by faith on shifting sand.

The tempest roars, yet still we stand,
With courage born from deep within.
Each wave a challenge, fierce and grand,
We trust the journey we begin.

His love, a compass in the storm,
Each color shines through darkest night.
With every drop, our hearts transform,
Alive, we dance in radiant light.

In every struggle, wisdom grows,
With hands uplifted, voices soar.
Together through the highs and lows,
We find the peace we seek for sure.

At last, we glimpse that promised land,
Where joy and grace forever dwell.
With faith, we clutch His guiding hand,
In harmony, we know Him well.

The Reclamation of Light

From shadows cast, we draw the flame,
In whispers soft, a truth is born.
Reclaimed the light, we rise, unchained,
In every heart, a brand new morn.

Each soul a spark, igniting fire,
Dancing through the realms of grace.
In love's embrace, we rise, aspire,
Together finding sacred space.

The burdens lift, the chains break free,
As unity becomes our guide.
In moments small, we clearly see,
The strength in which we all abide.

With every heartbeat, kindness flows,
In shared compassion, hope ignites.
We are the light that brightly glows,
The reclamation of pure sights.

With hands outstretched, we weave and bind,
A tapestry of love's design.
In every heart, that which is kind,
The light reclaimed, forever shines.

Epistles of Endurance

In the silence, a whisper speaks,
Hope unfurls where courage leaks.
Through storms that shake our very core,
We rise anew, forevermore.

Hands held high, we seek the light,
Faith becomes our guiding sight.
Each burden borne carries grace,
In trials, we find our place.

Hearts entwined in holy strife,
Through heartache comes the breath of life.
With every tear, our spirits sing,
In endurance, joy we bring.

Storm clouds break, the dawn is near,
In unity, we cast out fear.
A path of thorns, yet blooms arise,
In struggle, we find our skies.

So let us raise our voices high,
In faithful trust, we learn to fly.
The road is long, yet we are strong,
In love, we find where we belong.

Miracles Born of Brokenness

From shattered dreams, new hopes emerge,
A faith born deep, begins to surge.
In cracks of pain, the light shines through,
Miracles rise, a heart made new.

Through darkest nights, we seek the dawn,
In every wound, the spirit's drawn.
From ashes deep, rebirth will start,
Each broken piece, a work of art.

When faith is weak, love holds us tight,
In fragile moments, shines the light.
With open hearts, we mend and weave,
In brokenness, we learn to believe.

Joyfully, we dance on scars,
For through the pain, we glimpse the stars.
Each miracle, a thread divine,
In life's great tapestry, we shine.

So cherish cracks that let love in,
For from our sorrow, hope begins.
In each alchemy of life's test,
We find that brokenness is blessed.

The Canvas of Life's Trials

Life's canvas spreads, with colors bold,
In strokes of pain, the truth unfolds.
Each trial faced, a brush in hand,
Painting strength on shifting sand.

In hues of grief, we find our way,
Shadows dance, yet light holds sway.
With every challenge we embrace,
A masterpiece takes form, with grace.

When tempests rage and spirits wane,
The artist's heart knows deeper gain.
For from the storms, the stars will gleam,
In trials' depths, we find the dream.

Brush strokes wild, yet colors blend,
In every sorrow, love will mend.
The canvas grows, our lives align,
In each small moment, grace will shine.

So let us paint with fervent hearts,
Embrace each tear, where healing starts.
In every scar, a tale to tell,
On life's canvas, we all dwell.

A Testament of Growth

In gardens rich, our spirits bloom,
From seeds of faith, we conquer gloom.
Each trial faced, a lesson sown,
A testament to how we've grown.

Through seasons change, we rise anew,
In roots of love, our strength shines through.
For every storm that bends the bough,
We learn to yield, yet stand somehow.

With patience forged in summer's sun,
The journey speaks of battles won.
For growth is not a straightened path,
But winding roads, where we embrace the wrath.

So stand amidst the bloom and thorn,
In every struggle, we are reborn.
A testament to what we face,
In growth, we find our sacred space.

With roots down deep, we stretch our reach,
To share the love that life can teach.
In every moment, strong or meek,
The heart will thrive; the soul will seek.

The Soul's Pathway through Turmoil

In shadows deep the spirit wanders,
Bearing burdens, silent yonders.
Each step is steep, yet light does guide,
With whispers soft, the heart's abide.

Through trials fierce, it finds its way,
A flicker shines through clouds of gray.
With every wound, a lesson learned,
A fire within, forever burned.

The road is long, the path is wide,
With faith as armor, fears subside.
In every tear, a seed is sown,
The soul shall rise, it won't be lone.

In darkest nights, a star does spark,
Illuminating the gentle arc.
The guiding hands from realms above,
Bestow the strength to rise with love.

At journey's end, the soul stands whole,
Transformed amidst the trials' toll.
With gratitude for lessons tough,
A deeper strength, the healing buff.

The Dawn After Struggle

When night is long and shadows loom,
The heart will sigh, in silence bloom.
Yet hope does rise, like sun's first gleam,
A whisper sweet, it dares to dream.

In every struggle, grace appears,
Transforming pain to precious years.
A tapestry of broken threads,
Woven strong where sorrow spreads.

With each new dawn, the shadows fade,
The soul awakes, no longer afraid.
In golden light, the spirit thrives,
As faith ignites and love survives.

The morning sings a brand new song,
In joyful chords, where hearts belong.
With every breath, a promise made,
To cherish light where hope invaded.

For every tear that fell in night,
Unfolds a path to boundless light.
The dawn shall kiss each weary brow,
Renew the spirit in the now.

The Living Testament of Faith

In whispered prayers, the heart takes flight,
Through darkest days, it seeks the light.
Each step in trust, a story told,
Of courage fierce, and spirits bold.

With every challenge faced in grace,
A tapestry of love we trace.
In every struggle, faith is sown,
A living testament, it's grown.

Through valleys low and mountains high,
The soul shall soar, beneath the sky.
With open hearts, we share the load,
Together strong upon the road.

In trials faced, the truth unfolds,
In every moment, brave and bold.
A beacon shines, dispelling fears,
As love transcends, through all the years.

O'er every storm, the spirit sails,
In faith, we find what never fails.
A living testament, we sing,
In harmony, our souls take wing.

The Embrace of the Unseen

In quiet stillness, spirits dance,
A sacred bond, a fleeting glance.
The unseen thread that binds us all,
In every rise, in every fall.

Through whispered winds and rustling leaves,
The heart will know what the soul believes.
In moments hushed, the truth is clear,
The love surrounds, forever near.

Though vision blurs, we trust the way,
In shadows cast, the light will play.
With every heartbeat, grace sustains,
In unseen realms, our spirit gains.

Through trials faced, and fears embraced,
The unseen guides, our paths are traced.
In unity, we journey forth,
With open hearts of boundless worth.

In every sigh, the cosmos sings,
Of love that flows with hidden wings.
Embraced by faith, we stand as one,
In unseen bonds, our hearts have spun.

The Sacred Dance of Hurt and Hope

In shadows deep, where sorrows dwell,
The soul takes flight, through pain it fell.
With every tear, a seed is sown,
In silent nights, our strength is grown.

The fragile heart, it learns to sing,
A melody of love takes wing.
In hurt's embrace, we seek the light,
Hope's gentle glow breaks through the night.

When storms arise, we stand as one,
In unity, we're never done.
Together we weave, our stories blend,
In the sacred dance, we find our mend.

Through trials faced, our spirits rise,
In every loss, a grand surprise.
For in each wound, a tale is spun,
The sacred dance of hurt and fun.

So let us move, with faith renewed,
In sacred steps, our hearts imbued.
For hurt teaches hope, through every glance,
In the divine embrace, we find our chance.

A Testament of Healing and Happiness

In quiet whispers, healing flows,
A testament, where love bestows.
From brokenness, we start anew,
In gentle hands, our spirits grew.

With every dawn, a chance to rise,
A smile reborn, beneath the skies.
In laughter's embrace, we find our grace,
A journey shared, we find our place.

Through valleys low, and mountains high,
United we stand, our spirits fly.
A dance of joy, our hearts will sing,
In this testament, love is king.

Each step we take, a miracle gained,
In every loss, a lesson attained.
With open arms, we greet the fate,
In healing's light, we radiate.

Together we weave, life's tapestry bright,
In happiness found, our souls take flight.
With gratitude deep, our hearts will soar,
A testament of love forevermore.

The Hymn of Resilience

In murmurs soft, the hymn begins,
A song of strength, where hope still spins.
With every heartbeat, a rhythm strong,
In trials faced, we all belong.

The winds may howl, the tides may turn,
But in our hearts, the fire will burn.
Through storms we rise, unwavering stand,
In unity's grace, we lend a hand.

With every breath, we learn to fight,
In darkest hours, we seek the light.
Resilience sings, in every creed,
In faith united, we plant the seed.

As shadows fade, our spirits gleam,
In every challenge, we find our dream.
The hymn resounds, with voices clear,
In every struggle, love draws near.

So let us sing, with hearts ablaze,
A hymn of strength through all our days.
In resilience found, we stand in grace,
Together, forever, in love's embrace.

Beauty Born from Trials

In the depths of sorrow, beauty grows,
A tapestry we weave from woes.
Each tear a drop of sacred ink,
In trials faced, we learn to think.

With every struggle, a bloom takes flight,
In darkest corners, we find the light.
From ashes rise, in strength we trust,
The beauty formed from pain is just.

The heart, once shattered, pieced anew,
In every crack, a clearer view.
With hands held tight, we break the chains,
In unity's power, love remains.

Through tempest's roar, our spirits tower,
In every moment, we find our power.
The beauty born from trials shown,
In every path, we are not alone.

As stars align in the evening sky,
A testament of hope, we will not lie.
Together we rise, our spirits blend,
In beauty's name, our hearts transcend.

Strength Forged in Adversity

In shadows deep and trials long,
We rise amidst the strife so strong.
With every tear and every fall,
Our spirits sing, we heed the call.

Through storms that roar and tempests howl,
We hold the faith, we don't disavow.
Each burden borne, a lesson bright,
In darkest days, we find the light.

The scars we wear, a sacred seal,
Each hardship faced, our wounds will heal.
United hearts in struggle's dance,
We grasp the hope, we take the chance.

With prayers that rise like smoke on high,
We lift our souls, we seek the sky.
In every battle, courage grows,
A testament of strength, it shows.

And through the fire, we find our way,
A guiding voice, in night and day.
From trials fierce, our spirits blend,
In hardship's grasp, we rise again.

The Seraph's Turned Cheek

In the gaze of grace, where love abides,
A seraph stands, with arms spread wide.
When hurt is cast like stones so cold,
Their heart ignites a fire of gold.

With gentle words and open hands,
They turn the cheek, as hope demands.
Though darkness tries to claim the soul,
A brighter path will make us whole.

Forgiveness blooms in barren lands,
A true embrace that understands.
In every act of selfless care,
The seraph's light, beyond compare.

No malice held, no bitter sway,
Love conquers all, come what may.
With every moment, kindness sown,
In hearts anew, compassion grown.

For in the face of strife and pain,
A seraph's heart will still remain.
In turning cheeks, we carry forth,
To show the world our boundless worth.

Beneath the Veil of Sorrow

Beneath the veil, where shadows dwell,
A whisper lingers, soft and swell.
In sorrow's clutch, we search for grace,
As tears cascade, we find our place.

Through valleys low, our spirits tread,
Upon the path of those who've led.
With every step, our hearts unite,
In darkness found, we seek the light.

The burdens carried, they weigh us down,
Yet in the depths, we shall not drown.
For from despair, new blooms arise,
In grief's embrace, the spirit flies.

With hope as our eternal thread,
We weave our dreams, though filled with dread.
In unity, we break the chains,
From sorrow's grip, true strength remains.

So let the veil be drawn aside,
In love's embrace, we shall abide.
From sorrow's depths, we'll rise anew,
For in our hearts, the light shines through.

Joy's Silent Uprising

In silent whispers, joy takes flight,
A gentle spark in still of night.
With every breath, we find the sound,
As laughter blooms from hallowed ground.

Through trials faced, in shadows cast,
A joy arises, fierce and vast.
No more confined by chains of fear,
In every heartbeat, it draws near.

From depths of sorrow, beauty grows,
As hope ignites, the spirit glows.
With open hearts, we let love reign,
In joy's embrace, we break the chain.

With tender grace, it finds its way,
A silent uprising, come what may.
Together we shall weave the thread,
Of joy reborn, where none are dead.

In every moment, pure and bright,
We gather strength, we take to flight.
For joy, once hidden, now unfolds,
A radiant tale, in love retold.

Miracles in the Shadows

In the night, when silence sings,
Hope ignites on whispering wings.
Faith unseen, yet ever near,
Guides the soul through shadows clear.

With each breath, a gentle grace,
Carried forth through time and space.
In the stillness, miracles bloom,
Dispelling darkness, banishing gloom.

In moments lost, a spark ignites,
Filling hearts with radiant lights.
Though unseen, power pours,
Hearts awaken, spirit soars.

Trust the journey, seek the light,
Miracles lie within our sight.
Every tear, a story told,
A precious gift, a heart of gold.

In the shadows, beauty glows,
Grace abounds and love bestows.
Hold the faith, let spirits rise,
For miracles wear no disguise.

The Gospel of Unseen Battles

In the silence, battles waged,
Unseen struggles, souls engaged.
With every choice, a truth unfolds,
A gospel written, brave and bold.

Hearts in conflict, voices low,
Through the trials, hope will grow.
Faith, a shield in darkest night,
Guiding us toward the light.

With prayer's whispers, strength divine,
Courage rises, hearts align.
In the fray, we find our song,
A melody where we belong.

Every tear, a seed of grace,
In battles fought, we find our place.
United in the struggle's art,
We lift each other, heart to heart.

Though unseen, the battles rage,
We stand as one, we turn the page.
With faith unyielding, spirits free,
In each struggle, victory.

Cherished Imperfections of the Heart

In every flaw, a tale resides,
A reminder of the ways love abides.
Through brokenness, we find our song,
In cherished imperfections, we belong.

Each scar a mark of battles fought,
In the heart's embrace, wisdom's sought.
Real beauty glows from deep within,
Transforming loss to love's sweet kin.

Moments fragile, grace bestowed,
In empty spaces, healing flowed.
With every heartache, learn to see,
The sacred dance of you and me.

Unveiled truths in gentle sighs,
These imperfections, our greatest prize.
For in the cracks, love shines bright,
In our flaws, we find the light.

So hold your heart, embrace it whole,
Each cherished piece, a vital role.
In every shadow, joy will nest,
In imperfections, we are blessed.

Revelations of Joy through Grief

In the depths of sorrow's embrace,
Joy emerges, a sacred grace.
In grief's heavy weight, love is found,
Revelations bloom from hallowed ground.

With every tear, the heart expands,
Embracing loss with tender hands.
In the quiet, whispers grow,
Revealing strength through pain's flow.

Memories dance in the candle's light,
Bringing warmth to the quiet night.
Through the cracks, the light shines through,
In the darkest hours, love stays true.

From sadness blooms a radiant hue,
Transforming sorrow, making new.
In each heartbeat, echoes remain,
The joy in grief, a sweet refrain.

So let the tears fall, let them flow,
For in the hurt, love's seeds we sow.
Through revelations, hearts will mend,
In loss, we find joy again.

Benevolent Marks of Survival

In trials forged by faithful hands,
We rise anew on sacred lands.
Each scar a tale of strength and grace,
Beneath the light, our spirits embrace.

Through valleys deep where shadows lie,
The guiding stars above us sigh.
With every breath, His whispers call,
In unity, we shall not fall.

Threads of mercy, woven tight,
In darkened days, we seek the light.
With hope aflame, we walk our way,
Benevolent marks guide us each day.

With hearts aligned, we journey forth,
Exploring depths of boundless worth.
Each moment blessed, ordained by fate,
In faith we stand, our love innate.

So let us sing, our voices raise,
In gratitude, we share our praise.
For every trial we must survive,
With open hearts, we shall revive.

The Covenant of Enduring Love

In sacred vows, our spirits bind,
A covenant, both pure and kind.
Through storms that shake our very core,
Enduring love will always soar.

Hand in hand, we face the night,
With hearts ablaze, we find the light.
In whispers soft, our souls unite,
Together strong, our future bright.

As rivers flow and seasons change,
Our love, a bond that won't estrange.
Through trials fierce, our faith remains,
In every loss, His grace sustains.

With patience true, we weather strife,
In every heartbeat, love gives life.
The covenant writ in stars above,
A sacred promise, endless love.

So let our voices rise in song,
In every dusk, where we belong.
With faith as guide, our spirits roam,
Forever in His love, our home.

Elysian Smiles after Storms

From tempest trials, a dawn will break,
With every struggle, new paths we make.
In quiet moments, joy takes its flight,
Elysian smiles emerge from night.

As raindrops fall on thirsty earth,
Renewed we stand, rebirthed in worth.
With gratitude, we greet the day,
For in His arms, we find our way.

Through shadows cast by doubt and fear,
The light of love will draw us near.
Each tear we shed, a seed of grace,
In laughter shared, we find our place.

The sun will rise, the skies will clear,
In unity, we hold what's dear.
With open hearts, we embrace the morn,
Elysian smiles, from storms reborn.

So let us dance in radiant light,
With love and hope, our spirits bright.
For every storm we bravely face,
In joy we find our sacred space.

Holy Fragments of the Heart

In fragments found, we piece our soul,
With tender grace, we make it whole.
Each broken shard, a story tells,
In silence held, our spirit dwells.

Through trials faced, we learn to mend,
With faith as guide, no need to bend.
In every crack, His love pours in,
Holy fragments where hope begins.

With every heartbeat, we rebuild,
The love divine that keeps us filled.
In whispers soft, we find our way,
Through holy fragments, come what may.

As scars unite, our journey glows,
In unity, a garden grows.
Each moment cherished, a sacred act,
With holy heartbeats, we stay intact.

So let us share our stories deep,
In love's embrace, our spirits leap.
For in those fragments, bound so tight,
We find our truth, our endless light.

Tenderness Woven through Tribulations

In shadows cast by doubt's dark veil,
A whisper calls through the frail wail,
Each tear a seed in sacred ground,
From broken hearts, new strength is found.

Through storms that rage and tempests cry,
We gather courage, let spirits fly,
In every wound, a lesson lives,
With open hands, the heart forgives.

Embrace the path the heart must tread,
For in this journey, love is fed,
Each trial, a brush with heavenly grace,
Tenderness in the darkest place.

With faith as shield, we rise anew,
In unity, our spirits grew,
Through each tribulation's endless fight,
We find our peace, we seek the light.

Together we weave with threads of gold,
A tapestry rich, a story told,
For in the struggle, bonds are made,
A testament to love's cascade.

The Lifted Veil of Joyous Trials

When shadows loom, the heart will ache,
Yet in the stillness, hope will wake,
A veil lifted, revealing grace,
Through trials, we find our rightful place.

Each step may falter, yet we trust,
That joy is mingled with the dust,
In every struggle, blessings lie,
With open hearts, we learn to fly.

Through laughter shared and sorrows borne,
In every tear, new life is sworn,
The trials come, yet so does peace,
From every burden, sweet release.

With faith as compass, we embrace
The joyous path, the sacred space,
Through every challenge, brightly shines,
A light entwined in heart's designs.

So let us dance in faith, rejoice,
For trials whisper a loving voice,
In every heartbeat, love prevails,
The lifted veil, the joyous trails.

Celestial Echoes of Resilience

In the quiet night, stars align,
Their twinkling light, a sacred sign,
Each echo whispers through the soul,
Resilience found, it makes us whole.

The winds may howl, the torrents rage,
Yet every page, a hopeful stage,
With courage born from deep within,
We rise again where we've been thin.

Our dreams like comets blaze the skies,
Each trial faced, a sweet surprise,
In every struggle, love ignites,
A flame that dances through the nights.

Together we soar, hand in hand,
In the light of grace, we take our stand,
For within us flows a river wide,
With faith as anchor, we shall glide.

As echoes of the heavens call,
In union strong, we shall not fall,
For life is woven with grace and might,
In resilience, we find our light.

The Sacred Tapestry of Life's Mirages

Life's tapestry unfolds in shades,
Of joy and sorrow, light evades,
Yet in the weft, the threads entwine,
In every moment, a grand design.

Through mirages seen in fleeting time,
We search for meaning, truth, and rhyme,
Each step, a stitch in fabric bright,
Guiding us through the darkest night.

With hands outstretched, we weave our fate,
In love's embrace, we elevate,
For every thread tells tales of grace,
In life's vast loom, we find our place.

So let us cherish the beauty rare,
In every challenge, learn to care,
For the sacred tapestry reveals,
Through every struggle, our heart feels.

Embrace the light within the weave,
In every trial, let us believe,
For life, though fleeting, is profound,
In our hearts, its love is found.

Joy in the Midst of Suffering

In shadows deep, His light remains,
A whisper soft, amidst our pains.
With every tear, a grace descends,
In trials fierce, our spirit bends.

Hope's gentle hand, holds weary hearts,
In darkest nights, new dawn imparts.
Through tempest's roar, we find our song,
In suffering's grasp, we still belong.

For faith, a bridge to brighter days,
In silent prayers, our souls ablaze.
With every wound, a healing grace,
In sorrow's depths, we see His face.

Embrace the light that breaks the gloom,
From ashes rise, new life will bloom.
In joys concealed, a treasure lies,
Through brokenness, the spirit flies.

So walk with hope, through valleys low,
In sorrow's song, His love will flow.
For joy emerges from strife's embrace,
In suffering's heart, we find our place.

The Alchemy of Adversity

In trials faced, our strength is forged,
From anguish raw, our spirits surged.
Each struggle met, a lesson learned,
In adversity, our hearts are turned.

The furnace burns, yet gold appears,
Through darkest nights, emerge our tears.
In pain, a beauty softly glows,
Transformed by faith, our spirit grows.

From bitter roots, sweet fruit can come,
In every storm, He makes us one.
With each setback, we rise anew,
In shadows cast, His light breaks through.

Through trials steep, we seek the divine,
In the depths of sorrow, His love will shine.
With every bruise, we learn to stand,
In crucible's fire, we find His hand.

So cherish pain, and wear it well,
For in each wound, His stories dwell.
In adversity's arms, we find our way,
Through every night, we greet the day.

Celestial Joy Amidst Earthly Struggles

Upon this earth, our burdens weigh,
Yet in our hearts, a light will play.
In every trial, a song we raise,
For joy divine, in struggles, stays.

When sorrows touch, our spirits quake,
His love, a balm, our fears forsake.
Amidst the chaos, peace takes flight,
In darkest times, we seek His light.

Each earthly trial, a path to grace,
In every tear, we find embrace.
With grateful hearts, we lift our gaze,
To heavens bright, where joy displays.

Through pain and strife, we learn to see,
The greater good in our decree.
For every struggle shapes our soul,
In joy's embrace, we find our whole.

So let us dance, in midst of grief,
In faith and hope, we seek relief.
For joy eternal, our souls will sing,
In every struggle, His love will cling.

Rebirth from the Ashes

From ashes deep, a phoenix flies,
In shattered dreams, new hope will rise.
Each ending marks a brand new start,
In life's great dance, the wounded heart.

With every fall, a lesson taught,
From brokenness, new strength is wrought.
The fire cleanses, the spirit heals,
In every wound, His love reveals.

In darkness deep, a spark ignites,
Transforming pain to holy sights.
As seasons turn, we shed the old,
In fervent dreams, our stories unfold.

Through trials faced, our faith grows bold,
In every sacrifice, love is told.
With open arms, we greet the dawn,
From ashes pure, new life is drawn.

So rise, dear soul, from sorrow's nest,
In your rebirth, you are blessed.
For in the journey, truth we find,
From ashes made, His love is kind.

Love's Echo in the Void

In silence deep, where spirits dwell,
A whisper calls, a sacred shell.
Through darkness spreads the light divine,
In every heartbeat, love will shine.

When shadows loom and hope seems frail,
The love within will always prevail.
In every tear, in every sigh,
Resides the strength to rise and fly.

Embrace the void, for it can teach,
The lessons love alone can reach.
In every loss, a new gain found,
In every silence, love's sweet sound.

Together we shall mend the seams,
In unity, fulfill our dreams.
For even when the paths seem lost,
Love's echo bears a holy cost.

So cast your fears into the sea,
Let love unfold, set your heart free.
For in the void, we find our way,
Through love's echo, night turns to day.

The Sacred Cycle of Healing

From ashes rise, a phoenix bright,
In each small step, we find the light.
Through pain's embrace, we learn to grow,
In nature's hands, we ebb and flow.

Forgive the past, release the chains,
In suffering, wisdom remains.
The sacred cycle spins anew,
In every heart, a healing view.

Beneath the scars, strength will bloom,
Transcending darkness, breaking gloom.
With every breath, a prayer we weave,
In faith, we trust, in love, believe.

Time's gentle touch will mend the tears,
In tender whispers, calm our fears.
Each wound a gateway to the soul,
In unity, we become whole.

The sacred cycle, life's pure dance,
In every struggle, lies the chance.
So let us learn, as seasons shift,
In love and light, we find our gift.

The Prayer of the Wounded

In quiet corners, souls mend slow,
With every heartache, seeds will grow.
Through pain, a prayer begins to rise,
A soft lament, a yearning sigh.

Lord, grant me peace in trials I face,
In the depths of hurt, show me grace.
Transform the sorrow into song,
In the embrace where I belong.

Whisper softly in night's embrace,
Remind me of Your loving grace.
For every wound, I seek Your light,
In darkest hours, be my sight.

Help me find strength in my despair,
In every burden, You are there.
Through struggle, I will rise and stand,
With wounds as badges, guiding hand.

In prayer I cast my hopes on high,
In brokenness, ignite the sky.
For every tear, a fleeting chance,
To trust in love's unending dance.

The Language of the Heart

In whispers soft as evening's glow,
The heart speaks truths that we all know.
Beyond the words, a bond so tight,
In love's embrace, we find the light.

With every beat, a story told,
In silence shared, our spirits bold.
The language felt, not always said,
In every glance, a path we tread.

In laughter's ring, in sorrow's grace,
The heart reveals its sacred space.
With open arms, we learn to see,
In love's pure gaze, we all are free.

Life's tapestry, woven with care,
In every touch, in every prayer.
Through trials faced, we come to understand,
The language of the heart is grand.

So let us speak in love's sweet tongue,
A symphony where we belong.
For in each moment, rich and rare,
The heart enchants, beyond compare.

The Blessing of Tender Scars

In every wound, a story starts,
Grace weaves through our tender scars.
With each stitch, a healing art,
Fragile strength forever jars.

The beauty of pain profoundly seen,
Emerging light in the broken sheen.
Forged by fire, each heart's serene,
A testament where we've been.

Each scar a verse, a sacred call,
The echoes of love in the rise and fall.
Embracing shadows, we stand tall,
With blessed scars, we share it all.

In the hands of time, we find our way,
Carried in grace, by night and day.
With tender scars, we choose to stay,
In the light of faith, we softly pray.

Forever marked, yet beautifully free,
Learning to dance in life's decree.
Tender scars, our testimony be,
In every heart, a legacy.

From Ashes to Radiance

In the darkest fields, where shadows strayed,
Hope ignites, unafraid.
From ashes cold, a new dawn laid,
Faith's embrace, our hearts conveyed.

Gentle whispers rise in the night,
Igniting dreams, a beacon of light.
Through trials faced, and battles fought,
In every loss, a lesson taught.

From the depths of despair, we rise,
With fiery spirits and open skies.
Emerging strong, no need for disguise,
In the warmth of love, our souls will prize.

Like phoenix wings, we spread our grace,
Embracing change in a sacred space.
From ashes we bloom, with life to chase,
Radiant paths, our hearts interlace.

In unity's glow, we find our peace,
A journey blessed, may strife release.
From ashes to light, our fears cease,
In love's embrace, we taste our lease.

The Faithful Canvas of Human Experience

Brushstrokes of life, rich and bold,
Stories woven, a tapestry told.
Each color speaks of sorrows old,
And joys that shimmer like pure gold.

In every heart, a canvas stretched,
With laughter's echoes forever etched.
Faithful strokes that life has fetched,
In moments cherished, we're truly blessed.

Canvas unfurls in the morning light,
Filling our spirits, banishing night.
With every struggle, we draw insight,
A masterpiece painted in love's sight.

Rich and vibrant, our souls adorn,
Amidst the chaos, new hopes are born.
In the faithful journey, we are sworn,
To embrace the beauty in life's mourn.

From shadows deep, we craft our fate,
In love's embrace, we liberate.
A faithful canvas, we celebrate,
In human experience, we resonate.

Whispers of Triumph in Tears

In silence, tears hold sacred ties,
Whispers of triumph beneath the skies.
Each drop a prayer, a love that flies,
In the depth of grief, hope never dies.

Through valleys low, our spirits soar,
With every sob, we yearn for more.
Life's storms may break, but in the core,
Resilience blooms, as hearts explore.

Tears that fall, a healing rain,
Washing away the weight of pain.
In sorrow's arms, we find our gain,
As whispers of love softly remain.

With every tear, a doorway swings,
To greater light, where freedom sings.
In bonds of spirit, our salvation clings,
In whispers of triumph, hope now springs.

From every loss, new strength we claim,
In the dance of life, we fan the flame.
Whispers of triumph echo our name,
In tears of joy, our hearts proclaim.

In the Light of Brokenness

In the depths of sorrow, we cry,
Seeking solace in the sky.
With every tear, a prayer is sown,
In brokenness, His grace is shown.

In valleys low, we find His face,
A gentle touch, a warm embrace.
Though we stumble, He lifts our gaze,
In light of pain, His love conveys.

Each shard of heart, a story told,
In shattered mirrors, truth unfolds.
With every wound, a lesson learned,
In broken paths, His light returns.

The weight of grief becomes our song,
In shattered notes, we still belong.
With each note played, hope takes flight,
In the light of brokenness, there's right.

So let us rise, though we may fall,
In His presence, we have it all.
With faith to guide us through the night,
We stand renewed in His pure light.

Hope's Radiant Flare

In the darkest hour, we stand still,
Waiting for the dawn, a quiet thrill.
With every whisper, hope ignites,
A radiant flare that shines so bright.

Through storms of doubt and fears that bind,
We seek the strength in hearts combined.
With every heartbeat, dreams take flight,
In the realm of day, we find our light.

Let the seeds of joy be sown,
In barren fields, where love is grown.
With open hands, we share our care,
In the face of wrong, hope's radiant flare.

Even in shadows, we feel the grace,
Of love that shines in every place.
With burning hearts that rise and share,
Together, we embrace hope's affair.

So let us sing of brighter days,
With every breath, we lift our praise.
In unity, our spirits dare,
Together we shine, hope's radiant flare.

Marked Yet Unbroken

Each scar a tale, a beauty untold,
In the book of life, our story unfolds.
Marked by trials, yet we stand tall,
In every challenge, we hear His call.

With hands outstretched in the pouring rain,
We find the strength in our shared pain.
Though we wander through the shadows cast,
In His embrace, we'll hold steadfast.

Marked yet unbroken, we rise anew,
With faith that guides and love so true.
In brokenness, we find our peace,
As wounds are healed, our courage won't cease.

Through the fire, our spirits bloom,
In every darkness, we face the gloom.
With every heartbeat, we claim our fate,
Marked yet unbroken, it's never too late.

So let us walk with joy unfurled,\nWith hopes and dreams to change the world.
In each moment, our hearts will sing,
Marked yet unbroken, in Christ, our King.

Grace in Every Line

In every verse, His love appears,
Bringing comfort through the years.
Each word a promise, whispered sweet,
Grace in every line, our hearts entreat.

Through trials faced and burdens shared,
In moments broken, we've always dared.
With every struggle, He holds our hands,
In the rhythm of life, together we stand.

With each breath drawn, His spirit flows,
A gentle whisper, as our faith grows.
In life's chapters, both dark and divine,
We find our place, grace in every line.

So we'll write stories of hope and grace,
With open hearts in this sacred space.
Embracing love, and sharing time,
Finding beauty in grace, in every line.

Together we journey, through storms and shine,
In light of truth, our hearts align.
For in our lives, by His design,
We find the peace, grace in every line.

The Song of the Stronghearted

In shadows deep, where spirits yearn,
Hope flickers bright, in hearts it burns.
With steadfast faith, we rise anew,
In every trial, we find what's true.

Each whispered prayer, a gentle might,
Guiding our way through darkest night.
With hands held high, we chase the dawn,
In love unbound, we carry on.

The storms may rage, the winds may howl,
Yet through the storm, we will not cowl.
In unity, our voices soar,
Together strong, forevermore.

A melody of strength we sing,
Each note a promise, life will bring.
In every heartbeat, courage flows,
The song of life, in us it grows.

So let us walk with heads held high,
With eyes aflame, beneath the sky.
For in our hearts, the light will spark,
The song of the stronghearted, our arc.

Threads of Divinity in Pain

In every wound, a story weaves,
A tapestry of what one believes.
The threads of sorrow tightly spun,
Illuminate the path begun.

Through trials faced, our spirits wade,
In every tear, divinity laid.
The aching hearts, a sacred tune,
In darkest hours, we find the bloom.

Each stitch of grief, a lesson learned,
In silent nights, the spirit burned.
With every ache, we rise and stand,
In threads of love, we understand.

The holy dance of loss and gain,
In every joy, there's woven pain.
Yet in this fabric, strength is found,
Threads of divinity wrap around.

Let us embrace the frayed and worn,
For in our hearts, the light is born.
In threads of pain, our faith will reign,
A sacred bond, through joy and bane.

The Silent Thrum of Resilience

In gentle whispers, strength will flow,
A silent thrum, the heart, it knows.
With every step, we rise and bend,
A journey walked, where shadows end.

Through trials faced, the spirit bends,
But like the willow, it never ends.
In quiet courage, we shall find,
The hidden paths of the divine.

Each bruise and scar, the stories tell,
Of battles fought, of rising well.
With hands outstretched, we touch the light,
The silent thrum, through darkest night.

So when the world seems torn and frayed,
Remember, love will never fade.
In every heartbeat, resilience gleams,
A silent promise, woven dreams.

Let strength arise from depths of pain,
In peace we'll grow, in love we'll gain.
For in the silence, hope will rise,
The thrum of life, where spirit flies.

The Mosaic of the Beloved

In every heart, a piece of grace,
A mosaic made in love's embrace.
Each fragment shines, with colors bold,
In unity, our stories told.

Through trials faced, we come alive,
In every struggle, we will thrive.
Embrace the light, the dark we know,
The mosaic grows, in love we sow.

With gentle hands, we shape and bind,
The treasured parts that souls can find.
In every crack, a beauty beams,
The mosaic of the beloved dreams.

Together woven, our hearts align,
In every moment, love will shine.
With painted strokes, we craft our tale,
The mosaic of love will never pale.

So let us cherish, each colored piece,
In diversity, we find our peace.
For in this oneness, we shall see,
The sacred work of you and me.

The Harmony of Healing

In whispers soft, the healing song,
The balm of grace where we belong.
Through trials faced and burdens shared,
In faith, our souls find peace declared.

Each tear that falls, a prayer released,
A journey vast, where doubts decreased.
The hands of time, they mend our hearts,
In love's embrace, the pain departs.

As morning breaks with gentle rays,
We rise anew to brighter days.
In unity, our spirits soar,
In harmony, we seek out more.

With every breath, a promise made,
In sacred spaces, doubts will fade.
Together we walk, a blessed throng,
In harmony's grace, we all belong.

From every wound, a strength we find,
In caring hearts, true love aligned.
With every heartbeat, hope resounds,
In healing light, our peace abounds.

Among the Ashes, We Rise

From ashes cold, our spirits burn,
In trials faced, a chance to learn.
Through darkness deep, the light will guide,
In faith, our hearts will not subside.

With every loss, a lesson gained,
In sorrow's grip, our strength sustained.
Among the ruins, hope ignites,
In courage wrapped, we brave the nights.

The phoenix seeks its place to soar,
Among the flames, we open doors.
Together strong, we rise anew,
In unity, our dreams come true.

With all we've faced, we stand as one,
In every heart, the battle's won.
Among the ashes, rebirth calls,
As dawn arrives, our spirit stalls.

In every shadow, light will gleam,
With every challenge, we will dream.
From ashes fine, our story writes,
In faith, we rise to greater heights.

Joy Reflected in Shadows

In moments dark, the joy takes flight,
Reflections soft, a guiding light.
Through trials fierce, we seek to find,
The love that warms the heart and mind.

Each shadow cast can show us grace,
In every struggle, find our place.
Amid the storms, we lift our song,
In harmony's arms, we belong.

With whispered prayers, our spirits dance,
In sacred spaces, a second chance.
In joy's embrace, the shadows fade,
In light's caress, our fears betrayed.

Together we walk, hand in hand,
In every heart, love takes a stand.
Reflections bright, in beauty shown,
In joy's pure light, we are never alone.

With every step, our souls ascend,
In love's true path, our hearts will mend.
Reflected joy, in shadows cast,
Through faith and love, we will outlast.

Sacred Wounds

In sacred wounds, the healing starts,
Each scar a tale, each tear imparts.
Through pain endured, we find our way,
In love's embrace, we choose to stay.

With every hurt, a strength will grow,
In darkness deep, the light we sow.
Though burdens heavy, hope will rise,
A healing balm, beneath the skies.

With open arms, we greet the day,
In every wound, a chance to pray.
Together bound, we share our scars,
In sacred trust, like shining stars.

Through brokenness, a truth revealed,
In every heart, our love's concealed.
With gentle hands, we guide the lost,
In sacred wounds, we bear the cost.

Yet from our pain, great beauty shines,
In love's sweet grace, our hope aligns.
Together strong, through every fight,
In sacred wounds, we find our light.

Divine Light

In every shadow, shines a spark,
A guiding star, when times are dark.
In whispered hope, we seek the way,
In faith's embrace, we choose to stay.

With hearts aligned, we walk as one,
In every storm, our race begun.
Through trials fierce and doubts that hide,
In divine light, we choose our guide.

Each step we take, a path divine,
In sacred grace, our souls entwine.
With every breath, our spirits soar,
In love's pure light, we find the door.

Together brave, we face the night,
In every heart, the spark ignites.
With hands held high, we lift our song,
In divine light, we all belong.

With open hearts, we share the flame,
In love's embrace, we're free from shame.
Divine light shines through all our fears,
In unity, we dry our tears.

Luminescence in Life's Crucible.

In shadows deep, a flame does glow,
In trials faced, our spirits grow.
Each tear a jewel, each wound a scar,
In faith, we find how bright we are.

Through stormy nights and sunlit days,
We walk in light, our hearts ablaze.
With every burden, strength we find,
In love divine, our souls aligned.

As gold is forged within the fire,
So we are shaped by true desire.
In darkness, hope lights up the way,
Guiding us through each testing day.

From ashes rise, the soul reborn,
A tapestry of love, not worn.
In every heartbeat, grace is near,
With each new dawn, we banish fear.

In life's grand scheme, we see our role,
To shine with love, to heal the soul.
With every struggle, heaven calls,
In unity, we break our walls.

Whispers of Resilience

Through the valleys, soft winds sigh,
Whispers of strength that never die.
With every heartbeat, courage speaks,
In silent moments, hope it seeks.

When shadows loom and spirits wane,
We find the light in every pain.
A gentle nudge, a guiding star,
Reminds us who we truly are.

Firm in faith, we rise anew,
With heart embraced, the heavens brew.
Each setback's grace, each loss a gift,
In weary souls, our spirits lift.

The storms may crash, the tides may turn,
Yet in the heart, a fire burns.
Through trials faced, we come to know,
The strength within that starts to grow.

In unity, we find our song,
With every voice, we all belong.
Together rising, side by side,
In whispers soft, our hearts abide.

Light Through the Cracks

In fractured paths where shadows fall,
The light shines through, a clarion call.
With every crack, a chance to see,
The beauty born from what must be.

In hearts once broken, truth unfolds,
Courage found in stories told.
Through trials met and battles fought,
We gain the wisdom time has brought.

The sun breaks dawn in colors bright,
Illuminating darkest night.
Each ray that dances on the floor,
A reminder of what's worth fighting for.

When doubts arise and faith feels thin,
We gather strength from deep within.
For in the cracks, life's essence flows,
With every breath, the spirit grows.

Let hope arise like morning's glow,
In every heart, let kindness grow.
For in the cracks, we find our way,
Embracing light with each new day.

Grace Marked by Pain

In trials faced, we bear the strain,
Yet in our hearts, a grace remains.
For through the hurt, the soul takes flight,
In darkest hours, we seek the light.

Each wound a tale, each scar a sign,
Of love that flows through space and time.
In every struggle, lessons learned,
In gentle whispers, fire burns.

With open arms, we greet the day,
Embracing both the night and play.
For in this dance of joy and pain,
We find the beauty that will remain.

The heart may break, the spirit bend,
Yet in the cracks, love will transcend.
A journey rich in every hue,
With pain as guide, we become true.

In every moment, grace revealed,
Through trials faced, our fates are sealed.
In love's embrace, we learn to stand,
For in our scars, we find God's hand.

Healing Waters Flow

In quiet streams, the waters heal,
A sacred touch that hearts conceal.
Each droplet speaks of love divine,
In every wave, His grace does shine.

Let burdens wash upon the shore,
As healing flows forevermore.
With whispered prayers beneath the sky,
The soul finds peace, it learns to fly.

In every brook, His blessings dance,
Reviving life with purest chance.
A fountain springs where hope does dwell,
In Healing Waters, all is well.

From mountain high to valley low,
The rivers of His mercy flow.
He guides the heart through storm and strife,
With waters deep, He grants us life.

In quietude, we find our way,
Through sacred paths, we choose to stay.
His whispered song, a soft embrace,
In Healing Waters, we find grace.

The Blessing of Scattered Petals

Upon the breeze, sweet petals fall,
A gentle whisper, love's soft call.
In every color, grace does bloom,
A blessing shared dispels all gloom.

The garden grows with tender care,
Each fragrance speaks of hope and prayer.
In scattered hues, His mercy spreads,
Each petal dropped, a life it threads.

With every step, the earth we tread,
Is paved with blessings, softly said.
Through seasons change, their beauty stay,
In flowered paths, we find our way.

The sunlight kisses every leaf,
In tapestry of joy, our grief.
As petals dance on winds of fate,
We find our hearts to love create.

In nature's hand, His love bestowed,
The blessings flow, our spirits glowed.
In petals scattered, truths unfold,
The stories of His love retold.

Grace in the Face of Adversity

Through trials deep, our spirits rise,
In darkest hours, our faith complies.
With strength renewed, we stand as one,
Embraced by grace, our battle's won.

Through storms that shake and winds that roar,
A quiet voice will guide us more.
In every tear, a lesson learned,
In every crash, our souls have turned.

With hearts uplifted, fears erased,
We find the light in love embraced.
For when the night seems to outlast,
We shine the brightest from the past.

Each stumble met with gentle ease,
In every sorrow, we find peace.
Grace weathers storms, restores our sight,
In harshest dark, we seek the light.

With open arms, we face the night,
In every shadow, seek His light.
Through trials fierce, we find our song,
With grace bestowed, we shall be strong.

The Heart's Palimpsest

Inscribed with love, the heart's own tale,
Through joys and pains, it shall prevail.
Each layer rich with memory,
The past entwined with mystery.

With every stroke, the ink reveals,
A journey drawn, the spirit heals.
From broken dreams and whispered grace,
The heart's palimpsest leaves its trace.

In shadows cast, the light will break,
A canvas born in every ache.
Through trials faced, its strength bestowed,
In sacred scars, the truth is showed.

The love we weave through every tear,
Will guide us home, draw us near.
With every heartbeat, wisdom flows,
In every chapter, love's story grows.

Through seasons' turn and time's embrace,
The heart reflects a sacred space.
In every line, a sacred trust,
The heart's palimpsest, we adjust.

The Altar of Resilience

In shadows deep, we bend our knees,
With whispers soft, we call for peace.
The trials faced, a sacred rite,
In faith we stand, in love's pure light.

Through storms that rage, our spirits soar,
Each wound a mark, each scar a door.
We rise again, through pain we strive,
The altar's strength keeps hope alive.

In quiet moments, hear the cries,
The heartache shared, amidst the sighs.
For every tear, a seed is sown,
In resilience, our courage grown.

With every breath, a promise made,
In unity, our fears do fade.
Together bound, we face the fight,
On the altar of resilience, we find our might.

So let us gather, hand in hand,
To celebrate this promised land.
In faith we trust, our spirits blend,
On this altar, together we mend.

Beneath the Surface

In quiet depths, the hidden lies,
The soul's true strength, where silence cries.
Beneath the waves, the light does play,
A faith that's deep, a guiding ray.

The currents pull, the shadows sweep,
Yet in our hearts, the truths we keep.
Each struggle faced, a lesson learned,
In darkness found, our spirits burned.

When fear descends, a weight we bear,
Beneath the surface, whispers flare.
In faith we delve, through waters wide,
With hope as anchor, we shall glide.

So let us seek what's deep within,
The treasures found in every sin.
With every challenge, we emerge,
To walk with grace, our souls converge.

Together we rise, beyond the tide,
As dawn breaks sweet, our hearts abide.
Beneath the surface, love ignites,
In unity, we claim our rights.

Hope Glows

In darkest nights, a spark will bloom,
The whispers of the heart resume.
Hope glows bright, a beacon clear,
A promise held, forever near.

Amidst the storms, when shadows creep,
In fragile hands, the light we keep.
With faith as guide, we venture forth,
To seek the warmth that gives us worth.

Each step we take, a dance divine,
In every breath, a life we find.
With hope aglow, our spirits soar,
Together strong, forevermore.

In moments bleak, the light may fade,
Yet still we stand, unafraid.
For in our hearts, the fire glows,
A testament of love that grows.

So lift your gaze, embrace the dawn,
With hope as flame, we journey on.
In unity, our hearts align,
And hope will glow, a love divine.

Faith's Embers Illuminate the Heart

In whispered prayers, our souls ignite,
With faith's own spark, we face the night.
Embers glow within the chest,
A guiding light, our hearts at rest.

As trials come, our spirits bend,
Yet through the fire, we will mend.
With every trial, the flame will rise,
A testament that never dies.

In darkest hours, the embers gleam,
A flicker bright, a flowing stream.
With hands held high, in praise we find,
The light of faith, forever kind.

Through storms that howl, and shadows cast,
Our faith endures, our fears surpassed.
For in each ember, love does share,
The warmth of life, the strength of prayer.

So let us cherish, let us hold,
The embers bright, the stories told.
In faith's embrace, we light the way,
With hearts aflame, we greet the day.

A Tapestry of Trials and Triumphs

In every thread, a story spun,
Of trials faced and battles won.
A tapestry, our lives entwined,
In faith's embrace, our hearts aligned.

Each struggle sown, a lesson dear,
Stitched with courage, woven sear.
Through storms we wade, through shadows cast,
In every moment, the die is cast.

With vibrant hues, our stories blend,
In unity, our hearts transcend.
From pain to joy, the colors flow,
In this great weave, our spirits grow.

Together we share, both joy and tears,
Through laughter bright, and quiet fears.
A tapestry rich, diverse and strong,
In faith and love, we all belong.

So let us cherish, the beauty here,
In every stitch, a bond sincere.
Through trials faced, together we strive,
In this tapestry, we truly thrive.

The Pathway of Triumph

In shadows deep, we seek the light,
With faith as our guide, we rise in might.
Every step we take, a choice to believe,
In trials faced, we learn to achieve.

The road is steep, yet love will lead,
Our spirits soar, for we've planted the seed.
With every heartbeat, courage unfolds,
In unison, our story is told.

With hands reached high, we touch the sky,
In unity's strength, we learn to fly.
Together we chant, our voices as one,
The pathway of triumph has just begun.

Through valleys low, our hearts ignite,
With hope as our compass, we embrace the fight.
In moments of doubt, His promise we hold,
For victory awaits, in love's gentle fold.

The journey's essence, a sacred song,
We walk in grace, where we all belong.
Each step forward, a testament true,
On the pathway of triumph, we're born anew.

Beauty Born from Suffering

Amidst the trials, beauty does bloom,
In the depths of sorrow, we rise from gloom.
Each tear that falls, a seed of grace,
In suffering's arms, we find our place.

The scars we bear, tell tales of fight,
Of lost moments turned into light.
From ashes we rise, transformed and whole,
In burdens we carry, we strengthen the soul.

Like flowers in concrete, we learn to thrive,
In darkest places, we come alive.
Our hearts entwined in love's sacred claim,
Beauty born from suffering, whispers His name.

Through tempest's roar, we find the calm,
In chaos, we seek the healing balm.
Emerging from shadows that once felt so deep,
In trials endured, the promises keep.

With every heartbeat, hope ignites,
A symphony formed in the endless nights.
Each moment cherished, a glorious fight,
In suffering's cradle, we find the light.

Hymns of the Overcome

From valleys low, we raise our voice,
In hymns of the overcome, we rejoice.
Through stormy days, and shadowed nights,
We sing of faith, and soaring heights.

When burdens weigh, and trials press,
In unity, we find our blessedness.
With every struggle, our spirits rise,
In the heart of legends, our strength defies.

The echoes linger, of battles won,
With love as our shield, we stand as one.
In every note, a story we weave,
The hymns of the overcome, we believe.

For every wound, there's healing grace,
In boundless mercy, we find our place.
Together we rise, the fallen crowned,
In harmony's arms, redemption found.

So lift your voice, let the chorus soar,
With faith unshaken, forevermore.
In the journey shared, our spirits flow,
In hymns of the overcome, love will grow.

Echoes of Grace in Broken Places

In brokenness, His grace abounds,
In shattered dreams, new hope is found.
With tender hearts, we learn to heal,
In echoes of grace, we feel the real.

Each crack and crevice tells a story,
Of falling down, then rising to glory.
In every scar, a lesson learned,
In brokenness, the heart is turned.

The light shines bright in darkened hours,
In barren fields, behold the flowers.
Through trials faced, we reclaim our voice,
In grace unveiled, we make our choice.

From ashes of pain, a new dawn breaks,
In love's embrace, the heart awakes.
With every whisper, a truth we gain,
In echoes of grace, we rise again.

So gather the pieces, mold them anew,
In fractured lives, His love shines through.
In broken places, redemption's chase,
We find our strength in His embrace.

Rising from the Depths

From shadows deep, my spirit cries,
In silent prayers to the open skies.
With faith as my anchor, I reach for light,
And find my strength in the quiet night.

Through trials fierce, the soul must grow,
In waters churned, my heart will flow.
Each tear a sign of the burdens borne,
In hope, I rise with the breaking dawn.

The depths may hide my every fault,
Yet in the dark, new life will vault.
A phoenix found in the dusty grave,
Emerging strong, a soul that's brave.

Let every wound become a star,
Guiding me forth, though the path is far.
In gratitude, I lift my hymn,
For in the loss, the light is dim.

So here I stand, with heart in hand,
A witness to the great divine plan.
With humble heart, I seek to soar,
Rising from depths, forevermore.

Celestial Harmonies after the Storm

When thunder roars and heavens weep,
A silken silence gently creeps.
In chaos found, no fear takes hold,
For peace comes softly, pure and bold.

Beyond the storm, the skies do part,
Revealing beauty, a work of art.
Celestial light, in colors vast,
A symphony of echoes, from trials cast.

The world awakens, fresh and new,
Each drop that fell, a healing dew.
With every note, a heart does rise,
In sacred union, beneath the skies.

Though tempests rage at times in life,
They shape the soul through stress and strife.
In harmony, we learn to see,
The purpose deep, the mystery.

Let joy's refrain be sung anew,
In gratitude for all we've been through.
From storm's embrace, sweet lessons gleaned,
In every heart, the light redeemed.

The Lament of Renewal

In shadows cast by sorrow's hand,
A weary heart begins to stand.
With every sigh, a breath of pain,
Yet from the grief, new hope we gain.

For in the night, stars softly gleam,
Illuminating our deepest dream.
Each tear that falls, a seed of grace,
In nature's arms, we find our place.

This lament known, as time will tell,
Each hardship faced, a sacred swell.
In battles fought, we find our way,
Through loss and love, the heart must sway.

Let not despair shade every song,
For in our cries, we also belong.
In brokenness, we learn to mend,
In every ending, a new begin.

So lift your voice, let sorrow sing,
For in the pain, a blessing spring.
Each life a verse, in the world's rhyme,
In the lament, we find our climb.

The Heart's Scarred Landscape

Upon this ground, where silence lays,
My heart is etched in myriad ways.
Each scar a map of battles fought,
In woven threads of hope and thought.

The winds of change have twisted paths,
Yet in the journey, joy's warmth hath.
With every breach, the light breaks through,
In every scar, redemption true.

Through valleys low and mountains high,
The spirit soars, refusing to die.
In moments dark, the dawn will rise,
A testament to love's great tries.

Let nature teach us through the years,
That even pain can summon tears.
In every heart, a story laid,
In scars adorned, the love displayed.

So as we tread this sacred earth,
Remember well your spirit's worth.
For in our bruises, beauty gleams,
A landscape shaped by sacred dreams.

Milton Keynes UK
Ingram Content Group UK Ltd.
UKHW020040271124
451585UK00012B/970

9 789916 89896